AZU's Dreams of China
Hong Kong

Published in 2007 by
AZU Editions (Thailand) Ltd.
111 SKV Building, 8/Fl.
Soi Sansabai, Sukhumvit Soi 36
Klongton, Klongtoey
Bangkok 10110
Thailand

Tel: 66 (0)2 712-4016
Fax: 66 (0)2 661-2894
office@azueditions.com
www.azueditions.com

ISBN 978-974-8136-57-8

Printed in Malaysia

Global Consultants and Services Limited

Copyright 2007
AZU Editions (Thailand) Ltd.

All rights reserved. No part of this publication may be reproduced, stored in a retrieval system or transmitted in any form by any means, electronic, mechanical, photocopying, recording or otherwise, without the prior written permission of AZU Editions (Thailand) Ltd. All content, text, illustrations and photographs in this publication are protected by national and international trademark and copyright laws. Any infringement of the rights of AZU Editions (Thailand) Ltd. may lead to prosecution without warning.

For information about reproduction rights to the photographs in this book, contact AZU Editions (Thailand) Ltd.

Cover: *The Hong Kong Convention Centre seen from a sailing junk.*

AZU'S DREAMS OF CHINA™

Hong Kong

Photographs by Leon Schadeberg
Text by Michael Spencer

Shining
spires of glass and steel

soar amid verdant hills on the shores of the South China Sea; its distinctive skyline imprinted on our collective imaginations, Hong Kong is regarded by many as the quintessential modern Asian city. It is a place that inspires superlatives, synonymous as it is with boundless energy, wealth, and ambition.

Hong Kong's name translates as 'fragrant harbour,' which is derived from its beginnings as a Qin Dynasty port trading in precious incense wood. Since its founding, Hong Kong has continued to act as a bridge between the greater Chinese hinterland and

Previous spread: Victoria Harbour and the Hong Kong Island skyline as seen from Kowloon.

Left: Glass towers and red taxis are icons of the free-enterprising Central district.

the rest of the world – a role that it excels in and fulfils with even greater gusto today.

Home to seven million people of diverse Chinese and international origin, Hong Kong thrives on its contrasts and contradictions as a place where East and West meet and prosper. Since the handover from British rule in 1997, Hong Kong has become an integral part of China, but with its own status as a Special Administrative Region.

Contrary to first impressions, although parts of Hong Kong are among the most densely populated in the world, only 25 percent of its 1,190 or so square kilometres are fully urbanized, with much of the remainder given over to densely wooded hills, country parks, and nature reserves.

Made up of 262 islands, together with the Kowloon peninsula and New Territories

Below left:
Kowloon's Nan Lian Garden provides an oasis of calm for city dwellers.

Above right:
Verdant islands and vast tracts of forested countryside are a little known aspect of Hong Kong.

that are part of the Asian mainland, much of Hong Kong's topography is hilly and mountainous, characterized by a sinuous shoreline studded with bays, beaches, and coves, many of which are accessible only by sea.

The New Territories and large islands like Lamma and Lantau are parts of Hong Kong least explored by visitors, yet they offer a fascinating glimpse into rural China and its traditional villages, farms, and temples. The 100-kilometre-long MacLehose hiking trail that passes through gorgeous natural scenery and mountain landscapes is a must for outdoor enthusiasts, as are the Mai Po wetlands, where thousands of migratory birds congregate each year.

But the heart of the territory is Hong Kong Island, where a forest of skyscrapers in Central, the main business district, includes some of the world's tallest

buildings, dominated by the towering mass of the International Finance Centre. Drawn by what is consistently rated as the world's freest economy, Hong Kong is home to the largest concentration of corporate headquarters in the Asia Pacific region and the fifth largest stock exchange in the world.

For all its glittering towers, it is down at street level that the real pulse and raw energy of the city is best experienced. On the sidewalks, endless streams of people, who always seem to be in a hurry, flow in and out of shopping malls, restaurants, and office towers, or disappear into subway stations to be whisked off to other parts of the city.

On the main thoroughfares some of the world's best hotels, malls, and designer clothes and accessory boutiques all vie with each other for attention, while in narrow side streets, vibrant fresh-produce

Left: The Bank of China Building is one of Hong Kong's most eye-catching landmarks.

Above right: The best in accommodation and dining can be found at the famous Peninsula Hotel in Kowloon.

markets, traditional teahouses, and Chinese medicine shops from a bygone era lie waiting to be discovered.

At night the city loses nothing of its glamour as it becomes a sparkling wonderland of neon and glitz. Horse-racing under floodlights at Happy Valley amid an arena of apartment blocks lends a surreal touch, while entertainment zones like Lan Kwai Fong and Wanchai take on new personas after dark as they come alive with clubs, bars, and bistros that throng with revellers until daybreak.

Stately and dignified above the bustle, the majestic heights of Victoria Peak tower over the city. Reached by the Peak Tram, which ascends at a giddy angle through the Mid Levels, the park at the summit affords commanding views of the iconic Star Ferry boats linking Hong Kong Island with Kowloon and

Above left: Traditional junks, many converted as tour boats, can still be seen on Victoria Harbour.

Right: Causeway Bay is a shoppers' paradise for both locals and overseas visitors.

Left: The business district on Gloucester Road in Wanchai.

Following spread: Hong Kong's skyline is one of the most spectacular in the world.

its frenetic shopping districts and night markets of Tsim Sha Tsui and Nathan Road.

Hong Kong residents bring energy and intensity to all that they do, but nothing inspires them more than their love affair with food. From sophisticated fine dining in the top hotels and restaurants to outdoor food stalls, the bewildering range and variety of culinary options is a never-ending delight for the senses enjoyed by locals and visitors alike.

Hong Kong's lure as a global destination is firmly fixed in the world's imagination as a place everyone should experience at least once in their lifetime; it is a place like nowhere else on earth.

Left: *A reminder of the colonial past can be found in buildings like the Hong Kong Legislative Council.*

Above: *The clock tower near the ferry terminal in Kowloon.*

Above: *The Star Ferry has served commuters between Hong Kong Island and Kowloon for over a century.*

Right: *Hong Kong's trams are decked out in a rainbow of colours.*

Above: *The Peak Tram takes passengers to the top of Victoria Peak, 552 metres above sea level.*

Right: *Spectacular views of Hong Kong Island, Victoria Harbour, and Kowloon from the top of The Peak.*

Left: *The International Finance Centre is one of the city's most prominent landmarks.*

Above: *Skyscrapers seem to sprout from the greenery in Hong Kong Park.*

Above: *Martial arts such as kung fu are a popular activity in Kowloon Park.*

Right: *Hong Kongers always seem in a rush to do two things at once, even when relaxing.*

Left and above: Hong Kong Disneyland at Lantau Island offers fun and entertainment for all the family.

Left: *Visitors get a close-up view of the undersea realm at Ocean Park.*

Above: *Sea lions and dolphins are just some of the many attractions at Ocean Park on Hong Kong Island.*

Above: *Repulse Bay is one of Hong Kong's favourite beaches.*

Right: *Stanley, with its bars, restaurants, and market, is popular with expats and tourists.*

Above: *A village on Cheung Chau Island, typical of hamlets found throughout the territory.*

Above: *A lone fisherman in a creek at rural Tai-O, on the eastern side of Lantau Island.*

Above: The 34-metre, bronze Tian Tan Buddha at Ngong Pin on Lantau Island.

Right: A glimpse of ancient China can be found at the Lo Wai walled city in the New Territories.

Above: The walled entrance to the Man Mo Temple at Tia Po in the New Territories.

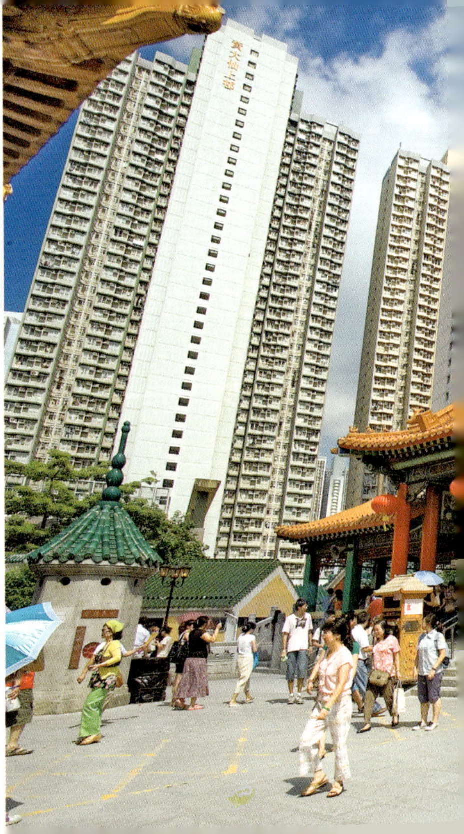

Right: Sik Sik Yuen Wong Tai Sin Temple in Kowloon is a popular place for city residents to worship and pray for wishes to come true.

Left: *An incense burner stands in front of the Che Kung Temple in Sha Tin.*

Above: *Fung Ying Seen Koon Temple boasts an elaborate interior.*

Left: *Chinese opera is still a popular traditional art form.*

Above: *Parades featuring dragon dances occur regularly throughout Hong Kong's festival calendar.*

Previous pages (left): *Hong Kong has no shortage of fresh-produce markets.* ***(right):*** *Kowloon's Temple Street Night Market dazzles with the array of goods on offer.*

Left: *Street stalls and open shopfronts offer a variety of freshly cooked delicacies.*

Above: *Dry goods and curiosities found at a market in Jordan.*

Left: *Striking displays add a splash of colour to the Festival Walk Shopping Centre.*

Above: *After dark, Causeway Bay teems with shoppers and revellers.*

Above: *Breakfast of tea and dim sum at the famous Lin Heung Teahouse in Sheungwan.*

Right: *Temple Street Night Market offers plenty of options for one of Hong Kong's favourite activities – al fresco dining.*

Left: Chinese medicine dispensaries offer curatives for all sorts of ailments.

Above: Jars of dried and preserved products at a traditional medicine shop.

Left: Hong Kong's streets are lively around the clock.

Above: Knutsford Terrace in Kowloon is a popular entertainment area for expatriates and visitors.

Hong Kong
Travel Facts

Where It Is

Hong Kong is situated on the eastern tip of the Pearl River Delta, downriver from the city of Guangzhou. Directly north is the Chinese border proper, the city of Shenzen, and Guangdong province, with the South China Sea on all other sides. Its geographical coordinates are 22 degrees North, 114 degrees East.

How To Get There

By Air
Chek Lap Kok Airport serves forty million passengers per year. There are about 700 daily flights on over eighty airlines to and from destinations all over the world, with numerous domestic and regional flights to mainland China. The Airport Express train connects to Hong Kong Station in Central in 25 minutes. There's also a 35-minute airbus service.

By Train
Cross-border rail services link mainland China with Hung Hom Station in Kowloon. There are three main routes, via Shenzen, to and from Beijing, Shanghai, and Guangdong.

By Road
There are four road crossings between Hong Kong and Shenzen; Lo Wu being the main link. A new Airport-Mainland Coach Station opened in 2003, offering over 100 bus departures per day to destinations in mainland China. Many cross-border bus services terminate near Prince Edward MTR Station.

By Boat

Ferries, hydrofoils, and catamarans provide links to Macau and Guangdong province. The airport has fast ferry links to ports in the Pearl River Delta. Locally, the historic Star Ferry operates four lines between Kowloon and Hong Kong Island.

When To Go

Hong Kong has a subtropical climate with 'summer' and 'winter' seasons. Typhoon season lasts from July to October, when the risk of moderate to severe storms is ever-present.

Winter, from December to March, is cool, often chilly, with occasional rainfall. The average temperature is 16 degrees Celsius, though it can fall well below this in the coolest month, January.

Summer, from May to September, is hot and humid. Sunny days are interspersed with overcast, warm days when sudden rainstorms can occur. Average temperature is 27 degrees Celsius, with July the hottest month. Eighty percent of Hong Kong's rainfall is in summer, with August the wettest month.

October, November, and December are the best months to visit; skies are clear, with plenty of sunshine. Travel can be difficult during the Chinese New Year in late January/early February. Other annual highlights include the Dragon Boat Festival in June and the Lantern Festival in September or October.

Find Out More

The Hong Kong Tourism Board's website at **www.discoverhongkong.com** provides comprehensive information.

Above: A performer in operatic make-up takes part in a street parade.

Acknowledgements

The publisher would like to thank the Hong Kong Tourism Board, whose kind assistance has made this book possible.

Authors

Leon Schadeberg is a British photographer who has been based in Southeast Asia since 1986. He has travelled extensively throughout the region documenting culture, travel, and lifestyle. His work has been exhibited frequently, both locally and internationally.

Michael Spencer is a travel writer and photographer based in Bangkok. He has travelled widely in Asia, Africa, and South America as a correspondent for a variety of international magazines and newspapers.